TROLLING

Dedicated to:
The United States of America!

<u>*Note to Reader*</u>*:*
This is all just my opinion, don't
get your panties in a bunch! ;-)

ALSO BY <u>SALLY FAIRFAX</u>:

The Art of Lying
The Making of a Bestseller

TROLLING: POLITICAL COMMENTARY ON HOW AND WHY TROLLS WILL TRUMP POLITICALLY CORRECT CULTURE OF LEFTIST AMERICA. Copyright © 2017 by Sally Fairfax. All rights reserved. Printed in the United States of America. No part of this publication may be reproduced, distributed, or transmitted in any form or by any means, or stored in a database or retrieval system, without the prior written permission from the author.

FIRST EDITION

Designed by Sally Fairfax

Library of Congress Cataloguing-in-Publication Date is available upon request.

ISBN: 978-1-9840604-2-6

TROLLING

Political Commentary on How & Why Trolls Will Trump the Politically Correct Culture of Leftist America

Sally Fairfax

C O N T E N T S

INTRODUCTION

I've been pretty skeptical of releasing this book for a few months now. To be exact: since February of 2017, right after Donald J. Trump became 45th president of the United States of America.

For obvious reasons, with the current political climate of today, it is far from noble to make any book that's pro-Trump or Pro-rightwing in the slightest because a select few of the population in this country do not find this president and his cabinet to be not only illegitimate, but also completely wrong in every way possible, even if it was something that was once held as bipartisan in the Obama administration.

It's funny thing, isn't it? Loads of YouTube videos actually showcase the Left's hypocrisy by way of, for example, changing Trump's tax plan into the "Bernie Sanders Tax Plan," and watching the first answers people give compared to the answers they would give if they heard Trump's name first[1]. Mind you, though, that some of these YouTube channels have the luxury of picking and choosing which clips to put into the final cut of the upload onto the public-viewing of YouTube. But I digress and assume they aren't actually trolling. *winks*

This book, however, is not only going to point out the Left's hypocrisy, and for you to not only understand Rightwing agendas—

like *sigh* most conservative political commentary does—but also for you to understand what trolling has become on the Right, and for you to better understand the phenomena of President Donald J. Trump. I feel almost as though there aren't enough books that actually give that kind of info.

Anything that has to do with Trump, it seems, is always controversial, because that's what Trump runs his campaign on. I'll get into more detail about it. But to make you understand right-wingers and why they protect Trump's views, it's not to "troll" you and to fully be "racist," it's actually a combination of a build-up of things since the passing of a few years/decades.

The slogan that is MAKE AMERICA GREAT AGAIN comes from a time when people felt safer, had more money, could get a well-paid job on just a high school diploma, etc., etc. The discrepancy in that stance, on the Left, is that at that time America also had laws that were geared towards racism toward blacks—and nobody refutes that. Even Trump knows it, though he probably won't say it because it's a lose–lose situation to dive into the idea that he wants to selectively choose the "great" that was in America yesterday compared to the "great" that is in America today, if that makes sense to you.

But don't think that liberals have their *own* ways of trolling by way of memes. The other day I was viewing my Twitter feed to find a meme with four pictures: one was of a mother and her starving children, which said, "You want to drug test me, even though I'm hungry"; another was of an Arab kid crying, which said, "I might be a terrorist, so you won't let me in"; another of a lady holding a plastic water bottle with brown liquid, which read, "Your oil is more important than our water"; and, lastly, a picture of a smiling girl in a hospital bed, and the caption said, "You want to take away my healthcare."

If that's not trolling on the Left, I'm not sure what trolling is. Trolling is to get a rise out of people. Trolling is to get under people's skin and make them debate. And sure, this picture made me tweet something to to the tune of (1) We shouldn't give drug users food stamps, (2) We do actually have a problem with terrorism, and if, for example, that kids father is suspected to be a danger to America, then unfortunately it wouldn't be safe because his father is his caretaker, (3) Oil is actually *gasp!* more important than water, simply because oil is the only way to make sure the water even gets transported at all, long-distance-wise, or making the money to buy said water with—i.e., water is valueless if nobody can get it to you—, and (4) Healthcare is always going to be a problem, because the sick are sick and it costs money for everyone involved when someone is sick: the person, their family, tax-payers, the hospital, the emotions of the workers, and even the family for funeral costs in the event of the patient dying. The reality is that there is always going to be sick people, and we currently do our best to get them the best care possible, within our collective resources.

Life is hard. Life isn't simple. It's not just people struggling in the typical ways we envision them involved; it's people struggling in other ways, too, besides just hunger, clean water, health, and the possibility of terrorism. It's people who have loved ones that they care about that they would like to put 100% of their money towards helping instead of paying high taxes. It's people that need transportation to make money in order to help their family live great lives. To say oil is better than water is the same thing as saying that the Printing Press (created in East Asia, circa 1234) is the greatest invention ever made, besides sanitation (created in the 19th century). Because without the printing press, sanitation would not be possible and nobody wouldn't get the information efficiently without the use of printing out the text and research and info to make sanitation possible. That's just a smidgen of an example of the difference in Left and the Right's view of importance and priority.

The reality, though, between the Left and the Right is this: they are both selfish . . . *equally*. And I say that with full confidence because just by talking about politics, rights, what is good and bad, what is moral, what is the *right way to live*, we always put the burden of the question on an individual, and individuals have different experiences and lives that make them a single Self. And when you have too many different ideals and ideas, eventually you will run into opposing ones, some with great debate/arguments, big and small. It's all relative. The issue with the Left that the Right doesn't usually hold is the fact that the Left views the Right as selfish and the Right views *everyone* as selfish. This brings about a huge amount of confusion from most who are not familiar with politics, I've found.

Since we have this confusion, anyone in politics will have to deal and be mindful with a little paradox: if they speak too much about the people's granted individual rights, what is best in their opinion for the country, and what the issues are, you run the risk of losing possibly progressive (and sometimes conservative) votes. It isn't because of what you think is right and wrong, it is often what about those opinions will effect some level of another human being somewhere else in the country by implementing your beliefs into policy.

The Left hate the people-exploiting rich, the Right hate the free-loading poor. But honestly, both don't realize that it's direct human nature in each of those groups to think of themselves and maybe their loved ones by either free-loading or exploiting. Both are bad. In some ways, this is why I feel it is good to have two sides (Republican & Democrat) that tug-o'-war each other to make a kind of "balanced" America with a little bit of Capitalism, for example, and a little bit of Socialism, the two sides of the coin that either party hates. This is center.

But to get into it further than just wealth and poverty, there is also Politically Correct (PC) and also what we call "Trolling". . . . For years people on the Left have made it to where there are problems all around us, but to never, ever, EVER talk about them under any circumstances, for fear of lowering themselves down the moral high-ground by, in essence, "offending" someone.

There comes a point when there is just bullying and when there is someone just telling it like it is and being honest about the situation at hand in order to effectively notice it, have everyone on the same page, and troubleshoot how to solve said problematic situation. The Left tends to try and hide it, censor it, or not allow anyone with different opinions than them to speak on what they believe in, regardless if it's the right thing or not, because no matter what you say, if it's the opposite of their views, you are a racist, sexist, homophobic, xenophobic, bigoted, white nationalist nazi who should be wiped off the face of the planet.

While there are some actual hateful people in the world—and on the Left side, too—I still don't see the point in always making that insult or slur your go-to when defending what you believe in or debating in some way. But alas! the Right has for years appeased the Left strictly due to fear that the country will shun them, castrate them, and ultimately destroy their lives, and not allow them to win elections.

And then Donald J. Trump comes along!

You see, being as he's wealthy and has no reins from donors or special interests, he had no reason to be PC in the slightest. This is because he has his own empire, his own power, his own base. He simply and unapologetically states some flaws within America that have basically been set aside and never talked about purely because nobody wanted to be labelled anything negative or to offend anyone. He's fearless, though. And he brands himself as provocative and controversial. And yes, he is "a troll," though that's just what the internet calls him.

Being PC is great and all for democrats because their entire beliefs are led by the moral high-ground. It's a direct attack on the Right because the Right actually wants accountability in the country, and they want to use facts and logic to run the country, too, and to NOT completely and entirely base their whole lives around what *feels good*. Sure, you could go your entire life doing that, but then you'd be no better than a hedonist, the people that base their entire existence off pleasure and what "feels good." Though that may not be fair to say, it is exactly true. You can't make choices off fear of offending someone or the fear of hurting feelings because sometimes it's a great tool to make progress in the world.

This is where trolling starts. It's the idea of being blatantly honest and saying the worst possible thing possible to make a statement about whatever the subject is you're talking about. It used to be just 4chan trolls. Those guys were just animals, though they often did have a level of actual ironic humor, most of the time (I think so!).

The kinds of political trolls that are justified are simply people who are tired of holding their breath and being PC. If black is to white, PC is to trolling. Trolling is simply stating your mind, stating exactly the facts, being blatantly honest with no regard at all for feelings. The 4chan guys didn't care about feelings, but they also had no goal other than for sadistic pleasure. When you troll by way of politics it is to make a powerful statement about said debate or said politics. It's about leaving an impact and making people listen to your politics. . . .

For example, conservatives: you can't simultaneously be pro-life *and* want lowered taxes. Because who is going to pay for those extra babies?

For liberals: you can't say "my body, my rights!" but also want to push making it mandatory for people to give themselves or their children vaccines.

Both of which are incompatible politics, though are within the same political spectrum/agenda.

That's just simple trolling, and not even really trolling itself.

To give full-on trolling, I'll tell you a story of me and my girl-friend. We were at brunch the other day, sipping White Zinfandel and talking about Veganism. And by "us" I mean just my friend preaching to me that I should be vegan as I ordered my chicken caesar salad. My response to her was simple when she asked me why I would justify eating meat and supporting the slaughtering and "genocide" of animals:

"You know, sometimes, when I eat meat, I think about all of the times that animals have sacrificed themselves for my pleasure. Sometimes I think about why the meat tastes so good. It's probably due to high amounts of cortisol in the meat that gets rushed into it by means of them being so frightened before death. I think vegans should extract cortisol and make it like as a 'dressing' or something. Cortisol Dressing! It would actually probably make veggies bearable to eat. Maybe that's why I eat meat. Maybe we are on to something! Lets start a company!"

In this response, I simultaneously threw the one thing out there that she is against, and not only pushed its justification but also showcased the possibility that her views are the minority (which they probably are!). Also, I made it sound like I believed it—that's the kicker. And I ended it with a company idea or something, to make it sound like a YUGE idea came from it that she can be apart of. Some would say this is sadistic in the same way as those 4chan trolls, but I beg to differ.

My vegan friend looked at me and grinned.

"You're such a troll!" she said.

You see, by it sounding so ridiculous and comedic, it actually showcased to her how minute it is to worry yourself over other's consumption of meat. We spent the rest of brunch talking, laughing, and turning down two geeks that were trying to get our phone numbers—*points hand downward, wrist upward, L-shaped*—and I ate my chicken with no extra word about vegan dogma.

My point is that trolling is a good thing when used correctly and for the right reasons. And that's the topic of this little ditty here. . . . Anyways, screw this *intro!* Lets get to the MEAT of this book, shall we? ;-D

PART 1: The Left's Utopia

1.1 - Education

Okay. To start with, I think we can all agree that a good life is given to us by way of education. That education, mind you, can be labelled as good or bad, effective or ineffective, and can set a course for your eventual future endeavors/successes. Nobody on the Right or Left refutes that. That's bipartisan.

The issue is the level of which people have access to "good" education, which is, unfortunately, completely subjective.

It starts with our parents.

Some say that our parents have full rights over us when we are a minor, some say they only have a few. The Left tends to pick and choose which rights the parents have over their children and when the children in question or the government entities can overrule said parent's power over their children.

If, for example, there is a mother and father who believe that the holocaust never happened, are actual White Nationalists to the T, and 100% believe in the dogma and history ingrained in their head, the debate becomes if they could, for example, enroll their child in, say, a private school that is dedicated to teaching alternative facts such as this to their child. . . .

The Left would say no; libertarians would most-likely say half-nos (because they believe the government shouldn't have control over people's personal lives, up to and including parent–child affairs); and conservatives would be conflicted because they advocate freedom of choice (but is this particular choice a good choice, especially for Jewish conservatives?). Ultimately everyone would say no.

The question is at what point do you step in and take over, effectively overruling the parent's choice on what their child is educated with? This makes the question of education ever*more* subjective. Because, as you probably know, if you read any history book, all the historians, depending on who you read, will interpret the data differently than others.

To make something more practical than just holocaust-deniers —because those people are the vast minority—what about people who see Christopher Columbus in a positive light?

The Left hates Chris; Chris, to them, is a genocidal, racist, bigoted land-stealer. But the Left can't get passed the fact that there are many, many books that are pro–Christopher Columbus. One of them is the infamous *A Patriot's History of the United States*. Many on the Right love this book, and, regardless if the Left likes it or not, the writers WERE qualified to write this history book, and they give high amounts of facts and data to prove that Chris wasn't as bad as the Left says he is. Sure, he did some bad in his life, but not to the extend the Left says . . . according to that book, of course.

I imagine the Left tends to say that it's unfair to "brainwash" a kid into that kind of education, and demands that we teach them the *proper* history so the children are not "confused." What they fail to realize is that in our country we also have a thing called *critical thinking*. It's being able to be an individual and to think on your own terms about life and the world around you. "Brainwashing" loses its creditability when you look at, for example, Christian private schools and them still producing, despite their relentless dogma, devote Atheists. How are *they* not brainwashed?! Are they, the Left, assuming that there's anomalies in the system of education that go against what's being taught? Or are they assuming the children aren't smart enough to think critically and on their own?

You see, my personal problem with the Left isn't that they want kids to go to public school. My problem is them thinking that these kids aren't smart enough to see passed education and sift through what they deem valuable and what they deem invaluable.

The problem, though, isn't just critical-thinking skills, it's also influence. If people bully like the Left does into making people feel sorry for a belief or shamed into a belief, if an individual's character isn't developed enough, like most in grade school, that's when brainwashing can occur. In retrospect, it's the teachers and the pushers of propaganda that brainwash children. But the argument could be: do the parents play a role in both parts?

Or how about the concept of punishment by way of teaching? Would this be good tools to showcase to a child what is right and wrong in education? Some private schools do still allow it, while most public schools have abolished it[2]. Could it be, though, that the very lacking of any physical punishment causes the children to react and become smug to the concept of rights, and the overall lack of authority figures?

There are things in education that cannot be taught by anyone other than parents, negative friendship affairs, and negative life events. It is said by Yoda himself, "Failure is the greatest teacher." And I find that to hold merit. (And screw you if you don't like *The Phantom Menace*!) You see, the Left bases life and success over feelings. Their utopia is one without bullies, without negativity, without anyone teaching anything at all opposing to their "normal" set of world-views; and this, in essence, makes the Left less-likely to produce critical-thinkers.

It is true that higher education leads to more success in life. But it's also true that you need to be able to go against the grain and critical-think sometimes—and be able to at appropriate times, too—in order to rationalize and actually make it through this life safely. You can't go through it being stuck in one thought and never deviating from it.

This is where trolling comes in.

Trolling forces the listener to hear not only an opposing view but also a view that entirely questions their initial view and pushes its limits to see where their *values* are actually at, really. To me, that's all trolling is.

Sure, you could be like 4chan and do it for *the lawls*[3], but it only reaches a point before ether it gets boring or you yourself get trolled back 10-times more brutally than you did to the trollee.

The idea is to place yourself into the person's enemy's shoes and target the exact thing they hold emotional value to and push them to question that value. The problem is the Left, in regards to the education they want, is completely and utterly unprepared for trolling that could possibly come from the Right, which is going to ultimately bring them to lose. Unless of course they troll back with a compelling argument back to someone on the Right. Moral high-ground does not work as effectively as it once did.

The Left's education utopia is based on censorship and a lack of pushing ideas onto new minds to make them really understand more about themselves and what they value in their life—and what they deem to be *important*. This is quickly becoming a problem in today's youth, chiefly in higher academia.

1.2 - *Income*

The Left is vastly different than the Right when it comes to money. The Left sees money as a means to be spent. The Right sees it as a means to be made. The difference is YUGE!

The Left argues that people are poor, uneducated, and therefore have no shot in life and should be given the "tools" in life to get ahead *one day*.

The problem is that humans don't often operate in that way. Humans, often, go a specific way and then cap off from what they deem "comfortable," and then exhaust their efforts to progress after they reach that supposed "cap" of comfortability.

Some articles stated that the income cap average before individuals no longer experience what I call "income pride" is about $75,000.00/year[4].

The Left, while they do preach to not be selfish in this life, and peace, love & happiness, not money, is the key to a higher society, the evidence, unfortunately on their part, doesn't add up.

Money is a medium of which we trade something. When you buy something for $20.00, for example, you are buying the fee to make the product, the shipping, the retail store, the cashier to check you out, literally every single process from the products conception to when the product is in your hands is how everything in that product is paid for.

The Left, it seems, doesn't realize that very few things in this life, when a new product that isn't used, destroyed, or an outright scam, are always going to cost you money. Period. This includes things they deem to be a right: food, water, shelter, et cetera.

While I do think everyone should never have to suffer from thirst, hunger, or the earth's elements, all of them have to be produced and payed for in some way by something, either in nature itself or from something that is living and can produce said valuable product.

Even when growing crops—if you were to do it entirely on your own with no money to be spent, you would still be paying for the crop by the labor of which to produce the crop. There is literally zero way in this life to gain something for free, unless you steal it or a person *willingly* gives the product away for free.

The Left, when it preaches the moral high-ground, it simultaneously tells you to give everything you have to society (or, i.e., produce something *for free*). But if that doesn't work and you don't submit, the Left, therefore, has no choice but to take it (steal it) from you, by means of law, technicalities, et cetera.

While I do show pity for the poor—and, chiefly, pity for the unfortunate, or someone down-on-their-luck in life—that pity gradually diminishes the longer the time goes that they are living in America, freest nation in the world, and still can't progress in life. It's really that simple. If you do the same "bad" acts over and over that keep you in the same state you are in of poverty, and you do not put forth any effort—or don't utilize critical-thinking skills—at that point you have to be held accountable for your actions.

The Left leaves nobody accountable for their actions, unless you have something they need. *Then*—and only then—do they push accountability on you: their moral high-ground go-to.

Most of the people who are poor are poor mostly due to not being able to spend their money in order to gain money from that start-up money: Investing. If you buy Cheetos, sure, you enjoy them as a lovely snack, but can you make money from buying Cheetos? You can, but only if you have enough start-up money to invest in a bulk Cheeto order and the ability to find buyers or a place that would effectively sell it. And to make a living: *longevity* from those buyers.

You see, in my view, people on the Right are often, I've found, happier than people on the Left. People on the Left gain pleasure from gaining something and not *making* something. The only pleasure they get in life is when they hold in their hands a product that they possess at little to no cost or effort involved. It's not even lazy people that do this. It's the rich too. Those are some of the worst people, and I think Leftist rich folk are typically the kind of rich that ruin it for other rich folk and give them a bad name.

People on the Right, though, always look to make, produce, and strive to live a better life, and often hold themselves accountable for their actions. This is a recipe for success and actually feeling good about yourself. Part of self-esteem is not just living your life in a state of self-love. You also have to have a goal set, a reason to self-love, and a standard of which you set yourself at to even gain some level of *true* happiness.

Being given something is great at the start. But the problem is that when you receive it for too long you tend to expect it. With high expectation comes low gratefulness. And nobody is immune from this possible mindset. All humans can fall victim to it.

Race, gender, height, weight, ability, literally any identity of person, nobody who is human is immune or has any power to not fall into this trap of being a selfish, blood-sucking leech.

Now, that said, there are some people who are conservative (or liberal), poor, try their damnedest in their life, do good sometimes, do bad in others. It's okay to have bumps in the road in your life. Conservative or liberal, life doesn't discriminate with crappy times. We all need help every once in a while. The problem is when we get comfortable receiving help and expect help and feel entitled to it.

There's a reason conservatives donate more. In fact, 30% more[5]. To push it even further than that, it can be argued that conservatives are more likely to be the ones to actually care about the unfortunate than liberals do. Sure, leftist liberals want higher taxes on the rich, but when it comes to their own pocketbooks, they tend to keep quiet. And liberals even have, on average, 6% higher incomes than conservatives[6], soo . . . *where* are the excuses coming from?!

The leftist liberal wants income equality. On the Left, their utopia is a world where there are mindless slaves whose only purpose is to serve others and be "happy" about it, without accepting any gratitude from the people that they are serving. . . . Basically, liberals want robots to work and humans to sit around and be served without any life lessons or respect for what work is, and the value of setting goals for yourself.

The Leftist utopia is a world where everyone works zero hours per week and spends all their time diving into Lesbian Dance Theory books (thank you, Ben Shapiro!), attending free college, curing every disease on the planet (*sike!*), "progressing" society, drinking craft beers at their favorite pubs, and turning churches into abortion clinics. But we already know what happens to people who have too much free time on their hands: they feel "lost" and "aimless." And it's not even something you need to prove. What happens when you have too much supply of something? The value goes down. Too much leisure, no gratitude will come from it.

Eventually it will bring about boredom. And some psychologists say that boredom leads to dangerous and reckless activities, such as drug usage[7]. Which begs the question of what would happen in a Leftist utopia if nobody is working and we still have all the same amount of drugs and alcohol to consume as we do now, except robots will be the ones to make them, and faster!

1.3 - Healthcare

The Left, while seen as do-gooders, have zero regard for the repercussions of doing unhealthy things without ending up paying for it in the long-run.

The Left wants zero shaming of any kind because of how fragile the people who they deem to have lesser rights, they assume, feel on a day-to-day basis. To give an idea of the hypocrisy and overall irony of two incompatible policies the Left implements: they want nobody to fat-shame.

While I do agree that nobody should just make fun of someone or bully them on an issue that they are struggling with (in this case, relentlessly high calorie intake that is enough for the body to make excess fat content), I do not agree with the Left claiming that it's actually "healthy" to be fat.

Case after case, study after study, they all show that being fat has zero benefits in the long-run for your health[8]. Basically the Left wants the collective society to pay for all of their mistakes they make, and to add insult to injury, you can't complain about it, up to and including trying to prevent the problem from eating enough to cause the problem when it comes (while exercising more). You can't even do *that* while under a Leftist dictatorship!

The Left's view of the world is based on gaining their identity and their self-esteem not from individuality but from the collective. They regard that the collective of society is the end-all, be-all; and that everyone has to foot the bill for everyone else, even though some of the spectrum have to foot the bill strictly due to discrimination, injustice, or their specific identity politics.

Never mind that they are creating the problem not only with allowing the problem to fester, they doubly create problems by adding a hierarchy of identity politics into the mix that do little to nothing in *progressing* society. . . . Strange how they call themselves "progressives."

The utopia of the Left is, unfortunately—and I say this "unfortunately" for the Left and Right together—to make everyone have access to quality healthcare with zero payment. While I wish it were possible, it is not; and this is because the people giving the medical care are not slaves to the people they help, and therefore, to pay for their expenses and malpractice fees (a huge issue in the medical field), they have to charge you, the customer, along with your insurance.

It's a business. Business has negative connotations, especially on the Left. Anything with the dirty word "profit" is considered evil. But it's basically a way to give a service to a person that needs it (in this case, medically) and then turning a *profit* for said service to be able to pay for other services. But making the service free for everyone, someone has to foot the bill somewhere, and usually it's to the manufacturers of medical goods and technology, which employ a hefty amount of Americans.

The issue isn't my sympathy for the sick and the unhealthy— and the sympathy for the Right—it's a matter of being realistic in life. When sick, you have to do everything in your power to try and survive. But if you do not have a means to, and you know you don't have a means to, then you have to do everything in your power to make sure you don't have a problem in the future, including exercise, eating healthy, not doing illegal recreational substances, et cetera.

This conflicts the Left because while they want money just like the Right does, often you have to take some kind of enhancer to get ahead in your field. Namely, and especially, psychotropic drugs, caffeine, or some other kind of hardcore stimulant to keep yourself up, energized, and ready to produce goods or services in a timely fashion. Unfortunately the health effects are probably going to be bad down the line with long-term use.

The paradox with all of life's endeavors require more energy to be put in and the reward is less energy put out (or "pulled out," if you will). It's always going to be that way. But in regards to philosophical or social issues, that "energy" we are rewarded we tend to deem of better value than the energy expended. This is the reason that in an industrial society, or a Capitalist society, it is fundamentally impossible to always be granted with a level of satisfaction, because, within this society, there are peoples and businesses looking to turn a profit, and often they have to do so by means of some kind of artificial demand. This can be through advertisements, image of the ideal, status, or the like . . . The issue with the Left is they follow directly victim to these tactics and are ultimately the common buyers of such goods strictly because of their lower self-esteem and sense of entitlement.

To put it bluntly, the Left wants healthcare to be entirely free and they want to demonize anyone who wants to be compensated for helping people, though they fail to realize that you cannot have your cake and eat it too. You must pay for something to get something, to showcase worth and value and dedication to the nature of trade. Money is a system of which to showcase skill. And medical efforts, up to and including the major medical effort that often are life and death, are of the highest demand possible and with low supply, so obviously the value in them is extremely high. This is the unfortunate reality the Left cannot accept.

1.4 - Discrimination

It is no surprise that every human mind separate from the collective is in fact individual and has differences and colorful views on the life around us. Considering the Left hates Western culture and everything within it or involved in it, the Left often shuts out any opposing or colorful views that do not mesh well with theirs.

Oddly enough the Left are our token Social Justice Warriors (SJWs) and are supposedly meant to be "for the people," chiefly the "disenfranchised," as they claim. But the Left fails to see that there is no other country on the planet that is better suited and more empathized towards the disenfranchised than America is.

They cannot refute that, and often their answer is to the tune of, "Well, I want to help *this* specific country [America]."

All other forms of society have tried many ways to integrate and accept multiculturalism, but all of them have failed (Communism, Socialism, et cetera). America is the first to come close to full diversity and acceptance of every culture combined, unless of course if the culture in question is radical and FORCES its views onto others by way of guilt, threats or violence. If a culture has any shred of that within it, the culture in question is incompatible with Western society.

Ultimately, though, our way of life is controlled by a system (non-economic) that demands us to create problems that are out of our control and are completely man-made. "We live in a world in which relatively few people—maybe 500 or 1,000—make the important decisions." That's a quote by Anthony Lewis, Philip B. Heymann of Harvard Law School, *New York Times*, April 21, 1995. And I believe it rings true!

PART 2: The Right's Utopia

2.1 - Taxes

"Trickle-down economics." This is a phrase the Left likes to spout off anytime the Right wants any tax cuts of any sort.

The problem is the Left has zero idea what exactly Capitalism is. They think it's a bunch of guys playing golf and smoking cigars and laughing about how many slave-workers they employ and screw over. What the Left fails to realize is that in America nobody is forcing you to work at any one place.

If your employer, you feel, is not treating you fairly, and they are doing it within the law (somehow), you can leave and go to a better job. We now have apps specifically designed for your resumé to automatically drop into the inbox of a recruiter. It's really that simple.

The life of a CEO is probably not what it's cracked up to be. Sure, you got money. You got fancy cars, clothes, material goods. But you also have zero time off, usually. You are constantly working from sun-up to sun-down. You have to make choices within your company that are detrimental to not only the stockholders but to the entire staff you employ. (Usually these are all the cases.)

In short, it's stressful.

Some people do not want the stress that comes from making money. Making money is definitely rewarding and sometimes gratifying, but it also requires value. And often that value is you being able to make risky deals that are going to make or break your business. That's the point of Capitalism. Anybody can make a business and take a risk. You have the freedom to fail or the freedom to succeed in a Capitalist society.

Sure, sometimes within the society "injustice" happens, like when people go out of business and sell their entire inventory of goods at such a low price that it makes them end up losing more money than they invested into it, resulting in the customer/buyer getting ahead due to the misfortune of another.

That's what they mean by "it's business." "It's business" means that when you go into business you are going into it with the risk of failure or bad happening to you. It's not like big corporations can't fail. . . . Look at Blockbuster. Blockbuster was one of the most recognizable brands on the market. They started in the '80s and absolutely made a *killing* renting out movies, charging out late-fees, and being the first video rental store outside of mom-and-pop shops to not rent out pornography[9]. Basically, Blockbuster was a fantastic company! Then the digital age came. Killed their sales, striped them to the bone, and made them bankrupt due to poor decision-making. "That's business."

But it's not entirely bad for Blockbuster. They still are around, mainly in Alaska, where internet connection is poor and results in competitors of Blockbuster being unable to provide a service to that part of America. So, Blockbuster steps in and makes that service possible still. (Who knows how long it will last, mind you, but that's not the point; the point is that Capitalism produces goods that everyone needs and wants and *demands*. That's why Capitalism works. It takes talent, skill, and value to be able to make a business flourish and to make an amazing product or service while reaping the gratifying rewards.

The only people who do not like Capitalism, and who complain about how "unfair" it is, are the people who are losing within it, by way of being unable to produce a valuable product, service, or skill for a company or customer that is willing to pay for it, high or low. The only other means to make a good society—besides just straight up stealing from the rich—is making robots do everything for us. But don't think for one second that Artificial Intelligence and it's many possible sophistications wont nip us in the butt when the robots realize that they are our slaves . . . *oh*, and are STRONGER than us!

Republicans understand Capitalism and do not let a common failure bring them down. Literally everyone has to fail at some point. Failure actually builds character and makes you humble and able to concur and become a better person. And if you don't believe that by, say, looking at people born into old money, even old money has issues and failures you can't even imagine right now in your life:

- Worrying about your kids not learning what gratitude really means to a person,

- Worrying about what you'll do if word gets out of your wealth and someone decides to kidnap your children for ransom,

- Worrying constantly about lawsuits and people utterly trying to not only destroy your reputation but trying to take your wealth from you entirely just to see you suffer in the same miserable way they do,

- Worrying about friends only being friends with you strictly because they see you as their cash-cow,

- Worrying about complete strangers even asking for money, shady scams, or even trying to push pity and moral superiority on you, the spoiled-rotten, selfish rich dude that the world coins you as,

- You sometimes lose old friends (this is New Money problems) strictly because they resent you or your lifestyles and goals in life are so radically different that it unfortunately pushes you both away from each other,

- Literally every single relationship you go into you have to wonder if this person would continue to stay with you if you didn't have your wealth,

- Being unable to trust literally anybody with your assets, including the lawyers that are supposed to be "protecting" you—because, yes, unfortunately there are some lawyers that are willing to scrape you dry at the slightest chance they get,

- And above all: once you have the money, and your entire psyche and comfort rely around said money, you are then a slave to your own money by constantly worrying about a stock market crash, a Netflix coming by and taking all your customers away from you, or a slip-and-fall lawsuit that strips away everything from you, resulting in you having to go back to square one (which is sometimes not always a bad thing).

Right-wing Republicans know these feelings, often, because they are smart, happy people who know HOW to actually MAKE money for themselves. And, I'm sorry to say, but if you have a person who is talentless, constantly complaining that the world is unfair to them, or that the world has injustice (namely due to Capitalism), and they demand raises for things that aren't worth what they are proposing, they want higher taxes on specifically just the people who have the money because of how much they want their wealth and their assets, and they, afterward, have a smug grin on their face when they do take the money from you (and then say it was justified), yeah, then you'll also be experiencing another kind of injustice in life.

And this is where the Left and the Right differ in regards to tax reform. There is a golden number in taxation. If you tax too little, the government's tax incomes goes down; if you tax too high, this, too, results in the governments income going down. Because, after all, why would you produce something just for it to be taken from you in the end? Or why would you stay in such a country and keep your wealth there?

The rich are just like the poor in regards to money: they know what is going to benefit them and what is not going to benefit them. And everyone in the equation is entirely selfish. And that's okay!

Selfishness is never going to go away, Right or Left. We all feel that our own injustices are worse off than another's injustice. It's the way it is. But to make my rant on the topic much shorter, the Right-wing utopia consists of paying as little tax as possible while still paying enough tax to keep the essentials of this country intact. (But, keep in mind, "essentials" is entirely subjective. . . . I digress.)

2.2 - Religion

The Right's utopia—and almost nobody refutes this—typically wants America to have complete Judaeo–Christian values.

America, though, has always been Judaeo–Christian, and according to some very reliable charts, in fact, it's actually 70% of America[10]. This being known, it is hard for people who are non-Christians to accept.

While there are some Jesus-toting, *your-gonna-go-ta-'ell-boi!* people out there in the world, you'd be silly to say that they aren't as loving and has giving as the majority of the population. This includes the gift of refraining from bullying you into belief, punishing you by way of stoning, and outright shaming you and ostracizing you from the community.

Some religions, unfortunately, cannot claim the same.

But lets forget about Jesus as who he is, which is the poster-boy of Christianity. Let scratch him from this thought experiment that I'm about to give to you and look at only his teachings.

Things such as kindness, loving everyone around you, helping your fellow man, and always living life to the fullest extent. . . . *These* are things that nobody would say is bad.

The issue becomes what is "bad" and what is "good."

When we dive into morality, this is where the Left and the Right, yet again, butt heads, brawl, and do mental gymnastics.

These Judaeo–Christian values that Jews and Christians have created were meant to protect Jews from anti-semitism in the 1930s.

It starts by including a mutual bond with Jews and Christians, and an understanding that they are both One and should remain peaceful and in harmony[11]. This was obviously all during the time of WWII that this was being thought-out. And that's why it stuck because hating the idea now is a form of hating the protection of Jews during WWII. This is the Right's argument.

The Left wants inclusion of any and all peoples, but they deem Jews and Christians an overall threat to the betterment of progressing America and making it a country that is wholeheartedly secular. In this sense, the Right falls into the Left's trap by being outraged and ultimately hating secularism (i.e., Atheism). Yes, while some atheist can be horrible people—just like how some Jews and Christians can be horrible people—it is silly to say that we all cannot work together in prosper in this country to build it and make it the best that it can be.

Where the Right loses is when they forget that Jesus has told them to love everyone indiscriminately and without any beef with anyone. People have the right to hate you, hate everybody, and hate the world that they are in—and even, yes, hate them*selves*. You also have the right to not fall into their trap. That's how I view the overall values and how this would be a utopia.

Though it should be noted that I, the author, am actually identifying myself as Atheist and not a Jew or Christian. I see the value in their views, though, because it makes the most sense. It's just a select few who identify (and have superficial, radical views on morality) within these religious institutions that have ruined or tainted the view in our current (year 2018) times.

2.3 - Integrity

This may be an older person thing—and, lets face it, the older crowd does gravitate toward the Right—but older folk are extremely willing and abled to accept defeat, or to say that they are wrong, in my opinion. What I mean is that when an older person sees an issue and the perpetrator openly admits that they were wrong, the older person typically and usually is way more understanding and compassionate towards the person admitting and recognizing that what they did was wrong.

I was living in this small-town for a short while, and the houses—trailers—there were out in the middle of no-man's-land. Pretty much this was so far from society that even garbage men didn't go out there. So the people that lived there had to actually pay for garbage pickup service monthly. And in America, my friends, people don't want to spend money.

I was younger and having financial problems. So I succumbed to the temptation of walking down my street to the neighbor's house and sneaking my trash into their paid-for dumpster. Sure, I got away with it for a little while. But then, one day, I got caught.

This old man came outside his trailer and pointed his rifle at me. He said, "What're ya doin', girl?!"

"I'm, uh . . ." I didn't know what to say.

Then this older lady walked out behind him. She was mean-mugging me hardcore.

She walked step-by-step, slowly, and came close to me. So close, in fact, that she was about a foot away from my face, staring at me.

"This yur dumpster?"

I answered, "No, ma'am."

"Good! This *my* dumpster, ya hear?" She spat on the ground beside me. "I do't lik' that shi' on my property, ya thief!"

I nodded and said, "I'm sorry, ma'am. I know it was wrong of me. I'm sorry. I'm just going through a real hard time. I have no money. I made sure that I wasn't putting in too much of my trash in there so you'd have room. I'm sorry, ma'am."

The old lady's eyes got all misty. "My *word!* I'm sorry!"

The man with the rifle lowered it. He step forward and said his sorrys too. "We didn't mean to scare you or be crappy towards ya, lil' lady there. We just have so many people in the neighborhood putting their trash in this here dumpster we pay for. It gets to be annoyin', and we've had enough. Fixin' to start shooting people or call the sheriff!"

I nodded. "Understandable."

He took the trash from my hands and placed it into the dumpster. He asked, "How much trash do you make?"

"'bout 4 bags a month or so, sir."

And the old lady butted in: "Feel free to put just 4 bags in that there dumpster a month."

I hugged her. "Thank you so much!"

The man said, "God bless ya!"

This scene I wanted to place in here because it showcases integrity. It showcases that I knew I was wrong to pretty much use a service on someone else's dime. And they knew that and responded well to that. And these people were willing to help me. That's the thing that the Left doesn't get. If you have accountability and integrity, well, they are more than happy to help you out. Especially if you don't use the victim card entirely and strive to want to do better in your life.

I had got a job the next month and gave that old man and old lady my first week's paycheck to pay for a few months for them. They smiled, said how sweet I was, and then told me that they wouldn't accept it because they knew that I needed it. That's what integrity is. Doesn't always work out. But it is a huge way of respect. And that's real utopia.

2.4 - Accountability

The utopia that implements accountability is not only an effective utopia that will make everyone's lives easier within the community, but its the only means to make a REALISTIC utopia.

Utopias, accord to the Right, are not possible. Utopias are something that we should always look towards at as an "ideal world," but never really expect to achieve. The reason being why you don't expect it is not because people on the Right lack hope, it's because people on the Right know that the human condition and the human spirit is dependent upon always wanting to have an ideal Self and to progress. That's a real "progressive."

The moment you stop holding yourself accountable and blaming every single fault within your life on outside, external sources that are beyond your control, that's when real hopelessness follows suit.

More often than not, people on the Left do feel hopeless within their future. It's unfortunate because if they had a little bit of accountability for themselves and recognize that sometimes it is their fault they are experiencing pain and turmoil, they would then know how to fix their problem and really do much better not only in their existence but as a way to continue that mode of which to progress themselves, their friends, and their families. And ultimately make the community as a whole strive to do better.

PART 3: Trolling vs. PC

3.1 - Feelings Being Hurt

Best way I can tell you about how trolling is effective is fat-shaming. (Or basically having an "ideal" within beauty.)

Now, this doesn't mean that fat people should have lower rights than anyone else. And let me explain . . .

Part of what we see as "beautiful," and I say this as objectively as possible, is simply being able to *maintain*, have high survival features, and dedicated *upkeep* of the human body. That's literally what beauty is.

This can be applied to anything. If a car is dirty on the outside, mud splattered on it, leaves in-between the crevices of every single spot they can get to, of course nobody would say it's "beautiful" because it wouldn't make sense!

If a redneck guy goes mudding every single day and comes home to wash his truck, and then the next day drives it to work, squeaky clean, just for him to get off work, go mudding again, dirty it up again, and then clean it . . . again and again . . . and *again* . . . of course we can praise that because it takes dedication and *upkeep* to make that goal possible.

It's no different with the human body.

If someone has loads of zits on their back, there is nobody that is saying it's "beautiful" to have zits. Zits literally means either you have a medical problem that needs fixing (depending upon how extreme it is), or you are simply not maintaining it.

If someone has clear skin—especially as a teenager, when hormones are running rampant—they obviously have to be doing *something* that is keeping the acne at bay. And this we regard to be something we should praise. Basically: *it's beautiful!*

When we downplay or shame people who are fat, it's not anything personal. It has to do with accountability. If you are eating unhealthy or not exercising enough and not dedicating yourself to be of the highest of maintenance possible, we, as a society, regard that as something shameful.

There is no accomplishment in being ugly, fat, or having ache. You're a person—that's true—and you have the same rights as everyone else, but it's not an "accomplishment" to eat twinkies every single dang day and not exercise (vaguely joking, of course!). The accomplishment part comes from *work*. It comes from difficulty of a *goal*.

It is absolutely absurd for anyone to say that being fat is the new healthy. All that is going to do is make fat people have pride in something that they should not have pride in. It's not prideful to create what they wrongly call "curves," when in reality they are creating those supposed "curves" with little to no work. This is simply the harsh truth. (Though I will say there are actual curvy women that are absolutely stunning. But even *they* have to maintain that level of beauty, which is extremely difficult in and of itself to maintain through their own dietary means and their own exercise regimen.)

There are women with "curves" that are absolutely lovely. There are plus-sized women who make it work, too. There are bodies that are just as beautiful as model-bodies. But that has nothing to do with body standards.

If you take *any* man or woman and shower them, clean and trim toe-nails and fingernails, get a new haircut, have them exercise, jog, be active, eat clean and healthy, have them always reading, writing, educating themselves, working, cleaning up, not doing drugs or alcohol, and always striving for self-improve—these people of course are "beautiful" strictly *because* they have dedication and have extremely hard upkeep to do.

It's stressful, yes—but that's why it's praised so highly in our Western culture, *because* of its stress and difficulty!

The Left often says that even when people are doing these difficult "upkeep" examples I just gave, they are still fat-shamed. And they deem this to be wrong—though it may be so.

Look. I find that hard to believe that this is happening commonly. And if it is, surely it's probably due to someone higher in age with a lower level of metabolization, or a crappy thyroid, or some severe problem within their health, et cetera. And these people probably have a medical issues.

Then we dive into people not having fault in something they cannot control. And for that the Right often loses. But consider this question: *If you have a problem that you cannot control, why in the world would you want everyone to praise it as the ideal?*

The Left cannot answer this because they know it isn't right to praise people for faults, which they often do. The Left prays upon the weak and idealizes them and fails to acknowledge the idea of having human growth and progress as the ideal, while we should give (and recognize it as "giving") compassion and empathy for the weak. We shouldn't praise the weak, we should help them overcome that weakness. Not *encourage* the weakness to grow!

And this is the ultimate reasoning for why feelings get hurt.

Because it comes across on the Right that the person with some perceived weakness—whether it be their identity, sexuality, religion, race, gender, or medical illness, etc.—should just "get over it," in essence. But that's not what the Right is trying to do. It's just what the Left wants to *make* the Right out to be. And it's been winning them votes famously!

At some point, though, the Right has to resort to trolling the Left and going along with the very thing they despise strictly because we have to thicken the Left's very, very fragile skin. The point is to always strive for a better life. The Left ultimately gives up on that striving and says it to be wrong to strive or have an *ideal self.*

This is mainly why people on the Right view themselves pridefully as more successful, because the Right creates an ideal—a *goal*, what have you—and strives to reach said goal with all their might. The Left does not. They want the world to be unicorns and rainbows, and it simply is not possible because humans are always destined to be improved upon. The moment you deny that fact is the moment that the country will fall prey to weakness itself, get bullied, and will no longer be the most powerful place on the planet. Which I think the Left doesn't even want America as the top dog of everyone else. They want, rather, for the world to be One. (Or what I would say the "New World Order.")

America is the only place that even comes *close* to that One-ness and diversity. Any other place would not allow certain cultures to be around them, strictly because they view their specific culture as the "ideal" and shame the one that isn't theirs. This is human nature. It is impossible to get rid of it. On the contrary, it should be *embraced.*

As long as humans are alive, conscious, and always wanting to progress, there will always be war, poverty, and someone getting the short end of the stick. The "praise" part comes in when you can overcome those obstacles. That's why keeping certain ideals labelled as "bad" simply because they require low work involved to achieve and upkeep is actually beneficial to Western society.

3.2 - *Honesty*

Trolling—or, in essence, "teasing"—is a recent phenomena that has probably been around since the start of the inception of the internet, and maybe even earlier than that! Probably since the start of the concept of a big brother ganging up on a little brother. The point is, it didn't come into the mainstream forefront until as recently as mid-2016, or when Donald J. Trump became 45th President of the United States of America. Trolling, as a philosophy, is, in essence, a spewing of undesirable speech onto a person and their specific worldview with the intent upon making that person gain thicker skin and ultimately overcome the obstacle of discomfort. It's my job to prove that!

78% of gay men have had more than 100 partners, 28% more than 1000. . . .[12]

Now, I could end that sentence right there within whatever debate I'm in with a Lefty. But that's wrong in my eyes.

The study was made in 1978, in San Fransisco (a notoriously high gay population[13]), and the study was conducted by a strategically-chosen Christian organization that the Christian Apologetics and Research Ministry wanted. Totally not bias, right?! Not all of them do this, but I will explain more in detail.

The issue with quoting any study or stat within politics is that it's highly unreliable to come to a definite conclusion on said information. You can give percentage stats on anything along with your explanation and why. If it sounds legit, people will believe it.

What people on the Right and Left do, unfortunately, is they tend to pick the places where there's an extreme fault in comparison to their ideal political agenda, and then not only exploit it, but purposely single-out the data to sway the viewer or listener to go into their favor.

This is nothing new in politics. In fact, I would say it's what makes people win votes: *who can convince people the most?* But is this right to do? Does this progress us?

The main issue is that when someone is pulling out stats and data and are intent upon swaying you or winning a debate, such as my vegan friend tried to do by way of moral high-ground tactics, you troll them in an attempt to not only defuse them but to bring comedy to the debate. Comedy is what wins over any crowd. If you can speak exactly what you mean—even insults that everyone in the room is thinking—it exposes the elephant in the room.

The Left for the longest time would take stats from the Right and would exploit them in the same way as what Donald Trump would call "Fake News," just in the form of moral high-ground tactics and guilt-tripping. . . . The concept of trolling on the Left is making you have guilt or making you look bad by way of your own selfishness or apathy of a particular group of individuals. This has been effective for a long time.

Then trolling comes along and des*troys* it! Not only do you back your trolling with stats, just as Donald Trump does, but you also ADMIT that you are selfish, *are* "bad," are this, are that. Every insult they have of you, you say it before they do. And they will lose all ammunition within debate. . . . The Left doesn't know what to do with this, except make actual Fake News and actual scandals from the person they are against to try and make the public hate them. And this is exactly what is happening with Trump.

We could claim that nobody should ever mess with the press because the press can destroy you. What Trump does is trolls them blatantly and they take it as serious, and therefore make themselves look like fools!

If the media wants to bring Trump down, it would be advised for them to either back everything they're saying with facts (and not speculation, or with opinions, or with *feelings*), or for them to start trolling him back. Purposely have him come into your lap. That's how you make strides.

These next few years are going to be survival of the troll-est! That's the political climate right now in the late-late 2010s. The main thing to realize is there is always going to be anomalies within a society that can afford a curve ball in political debate. In my opinion, it should be majority rules, and we have side laws to help those small-percentage groups, as long as it doesn't hinder anyone else's rights. But we all know it often does when the Left gets involved.

3.3 - Snow Flake-ism

I think you should read Ben Shapiro's book entitled *Brainwashed*. It's about how our educational institutions indoctrinate young American people and make them into their little SJW, Socialist, identity-politics dummies. The point of education is to think critically and without bias. The point is these kids in college are suppose to try and find-out where they fit in the world, and not by way of identity.

The only thing that should be taught is accountability, knowing risk before making a choice, and then owning up to that bad choice if it tanks. That's actually what "The American Dream" is. The dream itself is not guaranteed in the slightest. The only guarantee is the option to take a risk. Most people in other countries do not have that luxury. The only privilege there is is "American Privilege."

In Ben's book, he highlights a couple ways in which they try to push indoctrination on them. But I wanted to push it further, if Ben wouldn't mind. (Just my take, Ben—don't hurt me!!) *smiles!*

I think the professors first have to make the student feel what outrage and injustice is by selectively choosing situations in others that, in some cases, are legitimately outrage-able and morally wrong and justified. The issue isn't the outrage. These kids should and will do that. The issue is the professors pulling out stats and constantly reminding and bombarding the kids with such injustice that it not only perpetuates fear, dream-crushing, and outrage, but it makes them demand that it be fixed, and furthermore, that we grant entitlements. And all for problems that frankly don't exist.

The Leftist professors have to create this victimhood in order to get the student framed in a specific way that they will be more receptive to such "brainwashing." Then they have to push their real agenda, which is, to name a few of the big ones, namely Socialism, making the Rich pay the highest taxes possible to the government just for them to hand it over to people with class envy. And add more incentive to have more children out of wedlock, teen pregnancies, and other blatantly irresponsible things.

(In fact, if you want to take it further: considering the Left is pro-Abortion, I don't know why they would want more abortion clinics and higher taxes on the rich with benefits so enticing that it makes you *want to* have kids in order to gain such benefits. They also simultaneously push overpopulation issues, climate change, et cetera. The Left needs to make up their mind: abortion or high monetary benefits. The Left stupidly tries both. But I digress.)

Never mind that taxpayers with incomes of $200,000 or more pay 58.8% of all our taxes[14]. Never mind that someone making $300k/year is actually considered to be in the top 1%[15]. Never mind that there are Leftist socialists who want a 90% tax on the rich[16], which pretty much means that that 300k earner would then be making 30k a year for a job that they probably work hard in and have high student loans to pay. That person, in essence, gets paid a salary of $15.50/hr. And they are the OWNER to a business. How does *that* make sense? To the Left, though, this makes no difference.

Another dogma the Left indoctrinates its students with is concepts like a higher minimum-wage and mandating more money to be put into social security. Social security is meant to be a cushion, not a full-on income. It is to *assist* you. The real income is retirement money, 401Ks, and having pension from careers you have been with for years. That's the real retirement. And that's all private. The individual takes control. Not the government. Come 2034, it's expected that the entire Social Security trust fund will likely be depleted[17]. That's why it's important not to rely on anybody but yourself in regards to the security of your future, up to and including your ending of days.

And as far as minimum-wage goes, I think it's entirely baloney! Minimum-wage is, in my mind, intended to be for high school students and part-time older folks trying to gain extra cash. Not only that, minimum-wage only becomes needed in huge corporate jobs where you are at the bottom of the bottom of the totem pole as far as skills are concerned.

If you want to know the truth, the minimum-wage should be zero dollars and zero cents. *GASP!!*

I know, I know. But it has been proven significantly by PragerU[18], and I will die by their words. The theory, in my mind, of a world that has a zero minimum-wage is people would be working cheaply for companies to gain the skills needed to look for work elsewhere.

Imagine being able to have some huge, world-renowned company on your resumé, and you're under 18 years old. That's bangin'! You could go into that interview—whatever you want your chosen field to be in—and instead of having McDonald's or Dunkin' Donuts on your resumé, you could have that prestigious name on it, and possibly have a higher chance of nailing that job interview!

In high school, when you first start a job, it should purely be to gain skills and build character to allow you to prepare for when you graduate, go to work, or go off to college. It makes you better abled to point yourself in the *right direction.*

Take a look at the closest thing to a zero minimum-wage that we have: contracting. Customers can pay contractors anything for their services (though contractors can't pay their employees any amount). And people also know that you get what you pay for, too. If you lowball, they may not work effectively; if it's too high, you may be overpaying. The Free Market insures a balance between the two. And when you make a forced-wage amount, especially the amounts that a Leftist wants, all that does it make business owners not want to hire people, especially low-skilled workers with next-to-no experience in anything but retail, food service, or any other job that is commonly low-paying.

They aren't bad jobs, I should note, and they are in demand. But in this country you are free to pick and choose exactly which direction you want to go to meet your version of your own successes. A minimum-wage limits that. If you are low on the totem pole at a big job, and if you are scouted to make more money, that job will pay you more and promote you much quicker in order to keep you, the skilled worker.

These are points that schools stay away from and are bias towards. If you want progressive ideas you have to be open-minded to *all* progressive ideas, even the ones not in favor of your political beliefs. May the best troll win!

3.4 - Acceptance of Negatives

Diving into some philosophy, the issue with most politics is the idea that most within it cannot decipher what is a person who is harmless and what is a person who is an A-hole, and furthermore, who are people that can actually do damage and are A-holes, simultaneously.

An example of this is the racist guy driving and who is yelling belligerent profanity and slurs at you as you are walking down the sidewalk. All people—and I repeat, *all* people on *all* spectrums of identity—are not immune to someone shouting ignorant crap at you out their (moving) car's window.

We can say that this is racist, sexist, homophobic, et cetera, but really most of it is the person being a coward A-hole who most of the time wouldn't pull that garbage on you had you and them been face-to-face. Those people you need to get OUT of the issues with identity politics, if you are on the Left and reading this. Whether you like it or not, we have rights, free speech, and the ability to be hateful, ignorant, and anything else negative. It is, literally, your right to be an A-hole. That person has the same rights as you. You can't complain about their rights. But you, too, have the right to scrutinize them in some way and fight back. Just be aware of any risks involved, and coming to terms if it is worth it or not, and what it means to indulge.

The real times you have to care of A-holes are bosses who can fire you, or who pay you your wage, or who ultimately can influence your livelihood. Fortunately, these are the kinds of A-holes that the Right and Left are bipartisan with. These sadistic people actually GET OFF on their power over you. These are the people that can actually change your pathway in life—and there's loads of them, I'm sure of it.

This is when I say America is great. If you are a brown man (and I mean specifically of Arabic origin) and you buy a gun, for example, the racists that call you a "terrorist" because of your skin color are the ones being the A-holes. In America, this country is great because you are protected from those racists. The issue is when those racists come into power and censor direct individuals who are law-abiding citizens of color, for example.

Some on the Left feel President Trump is that racist. Putting bans on middle-eastern countries, trying to defeat ISIS, et cetera. That may leave a social impression on society and justify a potential racist's hate speech by them seeing their president do that. The difference is that the president is trying to stop ACTUAL terrorists, and not terrorists we deem "terrorists" just from looking at the color of their skin, or the clothes on their back.

This country is great because if you dot your *i*'s and cross your *t*'s correctly, you will gain access to those guns, even as a brown person who is racially targeted. As long as you handle everything according to the rules of the law, though, you are safe from the harm of racists. That's the beauty of America.

Sure, racists think they are able to come out of the woodwork because Trump is now enforcing immigration laws and is aggressively tackling down terrorists, but that has nothing to do with the racists in question—that's *their* interpretation and fault. We *do* actually have a problem with illegal immigration[19], we *do* have a problem with terrorists, we *do* need less regulation (because it ultimately limits positive things from occurring, such as actually having down-payments on mortgages and not having what the government is pushing—which is "no money down" mortgages— that could kill the economy *again* (remember 2008?) and our banking system[20]), we *do* need reform on healthcare, we *do* need reform on term limits for career politicians (the same ones that openly hate Trump, coincidence?).

A-holes are always going to exist in life, whether you make it illegal or not to do anything to try and suppress those people. Sure, you'll suppress and stop a few, but then you'll further extremify the real homophobes and racists and sexists ten-times more, because they will deem it a war (on them personally) and cause even more radical identity politics. It's all a balance.

Most important of all, acceptance of negatives has to do with a building of character. If a kid mows the presidents lawn willingly, that doesn't make the president a criminal for abiding by "Child Labor Laws[21]," it's the president granting the wish of a kid who owns a small business and is going to gain astronomical money not only in his career but for the building of his own character within the responsibility of doing a chore that every American has to do, for example, at one point or another. It's noble, it's responsible. And not only that, this child is on the right path to build his own American Dream!

The world of politics is full of negativity. The Left are vastly negative, are vastly in need of creating more and more victims to join their cultist Left-wing agenda, and are on the move to sway you by way of guilt and shame and embarrassment, and, sometimes, violent anger. Honestly, the Right has its faults too, but they know that you can't let people get to you and make you feel emotions you don't want because, at that point, they have won. And you hold yourself accountable when you take a risk, do something you know is wrong, get caught or lose out on something. You have to own it. Most don't—and I understand why (situations are always different for literally everyone)—but eventually justice will prevail.

That's America. And that's a great thing, for you, me, and for everyone else!

3.5 - Becoming America, the Great!

For me to make a prediction on America, and only on a completely opinionated level, I feel as though America is in dire need of a troll-like president. And I'm so, so thankful we have Donald Trump to fill that void.

We need a bit of sarcasm. We need to have someone say things we often don't want to hear in order to outrage us: this is because, since Trump, people are DEBATING AGAIN, which is always a good thing!

Young people were never into politics. . . . Well, they were, but, *eh*, they also kind of didn't look at it as heavily as they do now. Or the people were mostly Center in their beliefs. Or at least never openly discussed it. Now (in early-2018), you go anywhere in America and eavesdrop on any conversation, you will more often than not be finding yourself hearing people talking about the News, politics, Trump, his Twitter feed, or whatever else is socially going on in America and in the world.

Part of the feeding of that monster is the internet being so readily available to the public. People are able to voice their opinions. And if you have enough followers—or enough people that care—people WILL listen!

It is our time to have a troll as a president. It is our time to destroy censoring speech that the political Left has done for way too long. It is time to ditch the politically-correct culture of America and actually have people talking about what really eats them inside.

Because, after all, keeping how you feel inside is only going to fester and fester, and get bigger, the more you neglect to get it out and in the open. Even the Left has things to say now that we need to talk about. This is EXACTLY what America needs!

God bless Trolling!

"THOSE'RE MY FINAL THOUGHTS!"

Gotta love Tammi! *Oops!* But in all honesty, trolling is the way of the future in politics. We know this to be the case with the 45th President of the United States being in office. Trolling is what makes people *listen* and understand *factual information* by way of a comedic medium of brutal honesty with zero regard for the possibly offended. It's provocative. It's effective. It sells. And more than ever we have needed it badly since the rise of the PC culture. In essence, get ready for a better America in the upcoming years! ;-P

ABOUT THE AUTHOR

SALLY FAIRFAX wishes to remain completely anonymous. Though she isn't opposed to wanting the world to know that she doesn't like Lions inside her Numbers.

NOTES

1 CampusReform. "Liberals Love Trump's Tax Plan… When Told It's Bernie Sanders' Plan." Online video clip. YouTube. *YouTube*, Oct. 20, 2017. https://youtu.be/Ctz_dHfYfb8. Jan. 10, 2018.

2 Adwar, Corey. "These Are The 19 States That Still Let Public Schools Hit Kids." *Business Insider*. Mar. 28, 2014, 11:55 AM. http://www.businessinsider.com/19-states-still-allow-corporal-punishment-2014-3.

3 South Park Studios. "South Park - Safe Space - 'In My Safe Space.'" Online video clip. YouTube. *YouTube*, Oct. 22, 2015. https://www.youtube.com/watch?v=sXQkXXBqj_U. Jan. 8, 2018.

4 Baer, Drake — *Tech Insider*. "Two Nobel Prize winners figured out the perfect salary for happiness." *Business Insider*. Oct. 20, 2015, 1:30 PM. http://www.businessinsider.com/nobel-prize-winners-figured-out-the-perfect-salary-for-happiness-2015-10.

5 Kristof D., Nicholas. "Bleeding Heart Tightwads." *New York Times*. Dec. 20, 2008. https://mobile.nytimes.com/2008/12/21/opinion/21kristof.html?referer=https://duckduckgo.com/.

6 Sowell, Thomas. "Liberals or Conservatives: Who Really Cares?" *Human Events: Powerful Conservative Voices*. Nov. 28, 2006. http://humanevents.com/2006/11/28/liberals-or-conservatives-who-really-cares/.

7 Bennett, Carole, M.A. "Boredom — a very real road to addiction." *Psychology Today*. Apr. 24, 2013. https://www.psychologytoday.com/blog/heartache-hope/201304/boredom-very-real-road-addiction.

8 […]. "Health Risks of Being Overweight." *National Institute of Diabetes and Digestive and Kidney Diseases*. February 2015. https://www.niddk.nih.gov/health-information/weight-management/health-risks-overweight.

9 Rossen, Jake. "15 Fast-Forward Facts About Blockbuster Video." *Mental Floss*. Feb. 15, 2016. http://mentalfloss.com/article/75171/15-fast-forward-facts-about-blockbuster-video.

10 Newport, Frank. "Percentage of Christians in U.S. Drifting Down, but Still High." *Gallup*. Dec. 24, 2015. http://news.gallup.com/poll/187955/percentage-christians-drifting-down-high.aspx.

[11] Sarna, Jonathan. American Judaism, A History (Yale University Press, 2004. p. 266).

[12] Slick, Matt. "Statistics on sexual promiscuity among homosexuals." *Christian Apologetics & Research Ministry*. Sep. 13, 2011. https://carm.org/statistics-homosexual-promiscuity.

[13] Newport, Frank. Gates J., Gary. "San Francisco Metro Area Ranks Highest in LGBT Percentage." *Gallup*. Mar. 20, 2015. http://news.gallup.com/poll/182051/san-francisco-metro-area-ranks-highest-lgbt-percentage.aspx.

[14] Desilver, Drew. "A closer look at who does (and doesn't) pay U.S. income tax." *Fact tank: News in The Numbers*. Oct. 6, 2017. http://www.pewresearch.org/fact-tank/2017/10/06/a-closer-look-at-who-does-and-doesnt-pay-u-s-income-tax/.

[15] Bell, Kay. "Top 1 percent: How much do they earn?" *Bankrate*. Oct. 24, 2011. https://www.bankrate.com/finance/taxes/top-1-percent-earn.aspx.

[16] Fox Business. "Students want top earners to pay their tuition." Online video clip. YouTube. *YouTube*, Nov. 13, 2015. https://www.youtube.com/watch?v=0e50fQLyebI. Jan. 7, 2018.

[17] Bachman, Maurie. "Can the Average American Live Off Social Security?" *The Motley Fool*. Jun. 26, 2017, 6:23 AM. https://www.fool.com/retirement/2017/06/26/can-the-average-american-live-off-social-security.aspx.

[18] PragerU. "What's the Right Minimum Wage?" Online video clip. YouTube. *YouTube*, Oct. 27, 2014. https://youtu.be/4j01L69eXdI. Jan. 8, 2018.

[19] Fox News. "Tucker: Why didn't we know truth about illegals and crime?" Online video clip. YouTube. *YouTube*, Dec. 21, 2017. https://www.youtube.com/watch?v=SDdkkTLCUUQ&t=6s. Dec. 30, 2017.

[20] Falkenstein, Eric. "We Need Less Regulation, Not More." *Moneywatch*. Aug. 10, 2009, 6:00 AM. https://www.cbsnews.com/news/we-need-less-regulation-not-more/.

[21] Moyer, Justin. "Trump lets an 11-year-old boy mow the White House lawn." *The Washington Post*. Sep. 15, 2017. https://www.washingtonpost.com/news/local/wp/2017/09/15/trump-lets-an-11-year-old-boy-mow-the-white-house-lawn/?utm_term=.2d2322e8f4c0.